To Calan, Emmett, and Nola:
you're kind of a big deal.
—NS

Library of Congress Cataloging-in-Publication Data available

ISBN 978-1-338-31465-6

10 9 8 7 6 5 4 3 2 1          22 23 24 25 26

Printed in China 38
First edition, August 2022

Book design by Keight Bergmann

From the NEW YORK TIMES bestselling creator of HEART AND BRAIN

# THE OCEAN IS KIND OF A BIG DEAL

## Nick Seluk

Orchard Books • New York • An Imprint of Scholastic Inc.

**OCEANS** are so big and so deep that people have only been able to explore a very small amount of them. These huge areas of water take up more than twice as much surface space on the planet as land!

The ocean is one of the most beautiful and mysterious places on earth!

How did the ocean say HELLO?

KRILL

It waved!

OCTOPUS

# SO, WHAT'S IN THE OCEAN?

### SALT WATER
The oceans are made up of salt water. This is different from the water you drink and helps keep the living things inside the ocean healthy.

### ANIMALS
The ocean is home to one million different **species** of animals! This includes animals as big as the blue whale and as small as a tiny krill!

### PLANTS
The oceans support tons of plant life, including seagrass, kelp, and algae. Algae produces almost half the world's **oxygen**!

SEA TURTLE

STARFISH

Many of the plants and animals you know about live close to the surface. This includes coral, seaweed, sharks, dolphins, turtles, and more! Up here in the **sunlight zone**, the ocean is beautiful and full of life!

Every animal in the ocean is part of a **food chain**. The food chain is a way to show how animals interact with one another.

In the food chain, large animals like sharks eat smaller animals like seals. Seals eat smaller fish and small squid and octopuses. Those smaller creatures eat tiny animals like shrimp, which eat plankton and tiny **microorganisms**. And plants and microorganisms get their nutrients from the poop of the bigger creatures!

OH HEY, GUESS WHAT?

A single drop of ocean water can contain thousands of plankton and millions of even tinier **organisms**. Wow!

PENGUIN

SQUID

Krill! This way!

BLUESTRIPE SNAPPERS

There are more than 500 million tons of krill in the ocean! Krill usually travel in large groups and are food to many animals, including penguins and seals. Even some very large animals like the baleen whale eat krill!

The ocean is its own **ecosystem**, living in perfect balance with its plants and animals. A forest is another example of an ecosystem with its own food chains.

Below the sunlight zone is the twilight zone! As we go deeper, the ocean starts to get darker. That's because light doesn't go through water as easily as it goes through air.

Although some animals in the twilight zone may seem familiar, there are many unique and bizarre ones as well!

OH HEY, GUESS WHAT?

As the ocean gets darker, some animals use something called **bioluminescence** to create light! It means their bodies use their own energy to make light instead of needing the sun. Wild!

LANTERN FISH

SWORDFISH

What's deeper than the twilight zone?

MORAY EEL

Even deeper is the **midnight zone**, where it's as dark as it is in the middle of the night on land. Here, you wouldn't even be able to see the hand in front of your face without a light.

Wow, I didn't know these animals were all down here.

Me neither. I hope we don't wake up anything too scary!

Watch it! I have my OWN light!

ANGLERFISH

OH HEY, GUESS WHAT?

In some parts of the ocean where it's cold, animals live near warm vents, which are areas of water heated by hot **magma**, just like from a volcano. They are called **hydrothermal** vents ("hydro" means water, and "thermal" means warm).

Animals in the deep ocean have their own food chain. They also eat crumbs and waste that float down from the sunlight and twilight zones!

Let's go even deeper!

Are you sure you're not scared? You seem scared.

Poop from above! My favorite!

GOBLIN SHARK

OSEDAX WORMS

SEA CUCUMBER

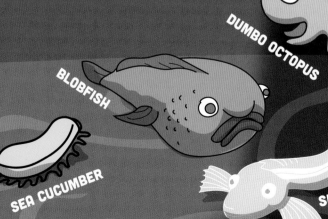

DUMBO OCTOPUS

BLOBFISH

SNAILFISH

Finally, the **abyssal zone**, the deepest, darkest, most mysterious part of the ocean. Here, animals really need those leftovers that fall from higher up. The water is so heavy that the fish have to move very slowly so they don't waste energy.

In the deepest parts of the oceans, many creatures are much larger than their cousins closer to the surface. Scientists call this "abyssal gigantism" or **deep-sea gigantism**.

Most sea creatures can breathe underwater, but animals like dolphins, whales, seals, and sea turtles need to come to the surface to breathe air every so often. They don't have gills to breathe underwater like most fish. Instead they have lungs, just like humans!

Looking at the surface of the ocean, it's hard to believe that most life on earth is under those waves. For humans, so much of the ocean is still a mystery, but we couldn't live without it.

What are those seals doing?

Those are humans, Krill. They're learning about the ocean.

Humans are always trying to learn more about the ocean. The ocean is very important to our life on land. The ocean provides food, medicines, and even affects the weather!

The oceans can hold a lot of heat from the sun. The movement (or **currents**) in the oceans shifts warm water to cold areas of the world, releasing heat and warming the air. That means oceans make a big difference in the weather!

The more scientists know about the oceans, the better they can predict what the weather will be like.

Some of the plankton in the ocean are called **phytoplankton**, and they produce most of the world's oxygen. Oxygen is the most important part of the air we breathe. These little helpers travel in huge groups and drift along with the currents of the oceans.

OH HEY, GUESS WHAT?

Phytoplankton use **photosynthesis** just like land plants! Photosynthesis is when a plant uses energy from the sun and carbon dioxide in the air to produce food for itself. During the process, it releases the oxygen we need to breathe.

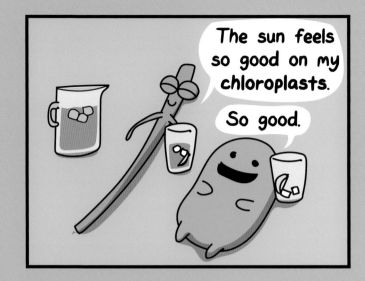

The sun feels so good on my chloroplasts.

So good.

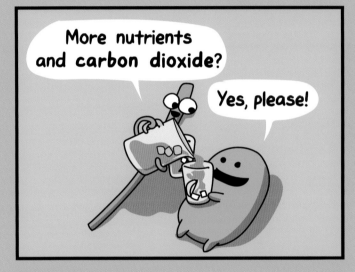

More nutrients and carbon dioxide?

Yes, please!

BURP!

Watch the oxygen!

Excuse me!

The oceans are great places to have fun, too. People love using the oceans for activities like surfing and boating, scuba diving and snorkeling, or just swimming.

**TOYS**

**NIGHT LIGHTS**

**PHONES**  **COMPUTERS**  **BOOKS**  **PLUNGERS**

**CAR PARTS**  **RUBBER BANDS**  **RANDOM CHARGING CORDS**  **PILLOWS**

In the United States, most things you get from the store crossed the ocean on a big boat. Oceans are how people get things like toys from the countries that make them. Many of your toys traveled a long way to get to you!

OH HEY, GUESS WHAT?

Traveling long distances over the giant waves of the ocean can be dangerous. Scientists guess there could be THREE MILLION ships at the bottom of the oceans.

The oceans have a BIG problem. Humans create so much garbage that a lot of it ends up getting dumped into the ocean. Most of it is plastic, which is bad for sea creatures.

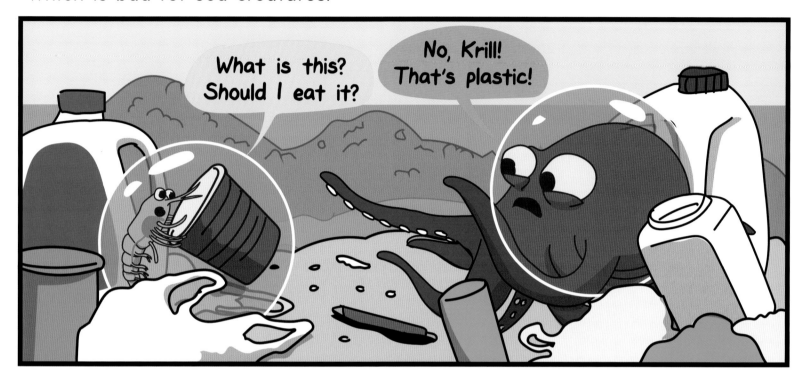

Plastic breaks into tiny pieces as it floats around in the ocean, which makes it easy for the sea creatures to eat by accident. That's a big problem for the animals, and could even become a problem for humans who eat fish for food!

Luckily, a lot of people (like you!) understand how important the oceans are, and they are working hard to fix the problem.

OH HEY, GUESS WHAT?

When something sits around for a long time, it **decomposes**. This means it breaks apart over time to be reused by the earth. Animals and plants decompose pretty quickly, but plastic takes a very long time to decompose. That's why plastic is a BIG problem.

I totally would have fixed it myself, but I'm glad they are helping.

Sure you would have.

Scientists are always looking for safe ways to get rid of plastic, but it's also important to use less of it.

There are many things we can do to avoid throwing away so much plastic. We can use things made out of materials that are better for the earth, like using paper bags instead of plastic ones. We can reuse items instead of throwing them away, and **recycle** anything we can't use anymore!

We can each do our small part to keep the oceans clean.

The oceans are huge, mysterious, and beautiful places full of really cool plants and animals! Oceans give us oxygen to breathe, food to eat, and even fun and relaxation. We wouldn't be able to live without them, and it's up to us to respect and take care of them!

NEEDLEFISH

KIHIKIHI

BUTTERFLY FISH

BLUE TANG

The oceans are one of the most important areas of the planet.

That's kind of a big deal.

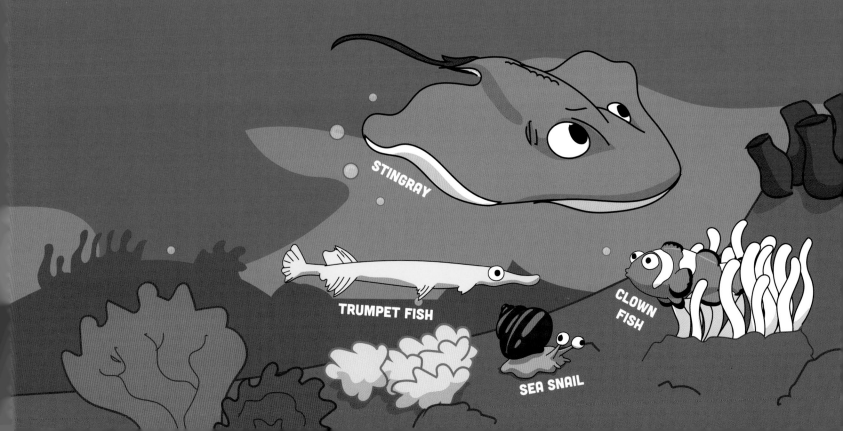

STINGRAY

TRUMPET FISH

SEA SNAIL

CLOWN FISH

# OCEAN FACTS

Kathy Sullivan is the first person to go to space as an astronaut AND travel to the bottom of the Mariana Trench, the deepest part of any ocean. Amazing!

The blue whale is the largest known animal on earth, and can grow to be 100 feet long and weigh 200 tons!

Coral looks like a plant, but it's actually an animal.

Meow.

The largest known shark was called the megalodon and grew to be 50 feet long, which is much larger than any sharks existing today. This fearsome fishy lived millions of years ago, along with many other unique animals—including dinosaurs!

The world's largest mountain range is actually underwater! The mid-ocean ridge is in the Atlantic Ocean and is over 40,000 miles long.

Scientists believe they have only discovered a very small percentage of the animals in the ocean. Who knows what other unique and bizarre animals could be down there?

# ACTIVITIES

## 1 WRITE YOUR ANSWERS TO THESE QUESTIONS ON A SEPARATE PIECE OF PAPER:

- What could you do to use less plastic at home or when you go out?
- What about ocean life is similar to life on land? What is different?

## 2 PICK AN OCEAN ANIMAL AND DRAW ITS FOOD CHAIN ON THE OTHER SIDE OF THE PAPER.

## 3 MATCH THESE CREATURES TO THEIR ZONE IN THE OCEAN:

Lantern Fish

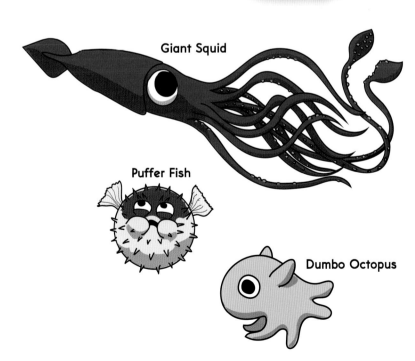

Giant Squid

Puffer Fish

Dumbo Octopus

Sunlight Zone

Twilight Zone

Midnight Zone

Abyssal Zone

# GLOSSARY

**ABYSSAL ZONE:** THE DEEPEST PART OF THE OCEAN

**BIOLUMINESCENCE:** LIGHT GIVEN OFF NATURALLY BY CERTAIN TYPES OF ANIMALS

**CARBON DIOXIDE:** A GAS MADE UP OF CARBON AND OXYGEN

**CHLOROPLASTS:** THE PARTS OF THE PLANT CELL IN WHICH PHOTOSYNTHESIS TAKES PLACE

**CURRENTS:** MASSES OF LIQUID OR AIR, EACH FLOWING IN ONE DIRECTION

**DECOMPOSE:** TO DECAY OR BREAK DOWN

**DEEP-SEA GIGANTISM:** THE TENDENCY FOR SPECIES IN THE ABYSSAL ZONE TO BE LARGER THAN THEIR RELATIVES IN OTHER OCEAN ZONES

**ECOSYSTEM:** A GROUP OF LIVING THINGS THAT LIVE WITHIN A SET ENVIRONMENT

**FOOD CHAIN:** A SERIES OF ORGANISMS THAT ARE EACH DEPENDENT ON THE NEXT AS A SOURCE OF FOOD

**HYDROTHERMAL:** RELATING TO THE ACTION OF HEATED WATER IN THE EARTH'S CRUST

**MAGMA:** HOT LIQUID MATTER RESIDING UNDERNEATH THE EARTH'S SURFACE

**MICROORGANISMS:** LIFE-FORMS SO SMALL THAT THEY CAN ONLY BE SEEN WITH A MICROSCOPE

**MIDNIGHT ZONE:** THE AREA OF THE OCEAN BETWEEN THE TWILIGHT ZONE AND THE ABYSSAL ZONE

**ORGANISM:** A SINGLE LIVING THING, SUCH AS A PLANT OR ANIMAL

**OXYGEN:** A COLORLESS GAS THAT MAKES UP TWENTY PERCENT OF THE AIR WE BREATHE

**PHOTOSYNTHESIS:** A CHEMICAL PROCESS BY WHICH GREEN PLANTS AND SOME OTHER ORGANISMS USE ENERGY FROM THE SUN TO TURN WATER AND CARBON DIOXIDE INTO FOOD—THEY PRODUCE OXYGEN AS A BY-PRODUCT

**PHYTOPLANKTON:** PLANKTON CONSISTING OF MICROSCOPIC PLANTS

**RECYCLE:** TO PUT THROUGH A PROCESS THAT ALLOWS THINGS TO BE REUSED

**SPECIES:** A GROUP OF LIVING ORGANISMS WITH COMMON CHARACTERISTICS

**SUNLIGHT ZONE:** THE AREA OF THE OCEAN AT AND JUST BELOW THE SURFACE, WHICH RECEIVES THE MOST SUNLIGHT

**TWILIGHT ZONE:** THE LOWEST LEVEL OF THE OCEAN THAT RECEIVES LIGHT